MIGHTY MACHINES

School Buses

by Kay Manolis

SCHOOL BUS

27

27

STOP

BELLWETHER MEDIA • MINNEAPOLIS, MN

Note to Librarians, Teachers, and Parents:

Blastoff! Readers are carefully developed by literacy experts and combine standards-based content with developmentally appropriate text.

Level 1 provides the most support through repetition of high-frequency words, light text, predictable sentence patterns, and strong visual support.

Level 2 offers early readers a bit more challenge through varied simple sentences, increased text load, and less repetition of high-frequency words.

Level 3 advances early-fluent readers toward fluency through increased text and concept load, less reliance on visuals, longer sentences, and more literary language.

Level 4 builds reading stamina by providing more text per page, increased use of punctuation, greater variation in sentence patterns, and increasingly challenging vocabulary.

Level 5 encourages children to move from "learning to read" to "reading to learn" by providing even more text, varied writing styles, and less familiar topics.

Whichever book is right for your reader, Blastoff! Readers are the perfect books to build confidence and encourage a love of reading that will last a lifetime!

This edition first published in 2009 by Bellwether Media.

No part of this publication may be reproduced in whole or in part without written permission of the publisher. For information regarding permission, write to Bellwether Media Inc., Attention: Permissions Department, Post Office Box 19349, Minneapolis, MN 55419.

Library of Congress Cataloging-in-Publication Data
Manolis, Kay.
 School buses / by Kay Manolis.
   p. cm. – (Blastoff! readers. Mighty machines)
 Includes bibliographical references and index.
 Summary: "Simple text and full color photographs introduce young readers to school buses. Intended for students in kindergarten through third grade"–Provided by publisher.
  ISBN-13: 978-1-60014-180-5 (hardcover : alk. paper)
  ISBN-10: 1-60014-180-3 (hardcover : alk. paper)
 1. School buses–Juvenile literature. 2. School children–Transportation–Juvenile literature. I. Title.
 TL232.M2838 2009
  629.222'33–dc22   2008012232

Contents

A school bus is a big machine. It can bring students to and from school.

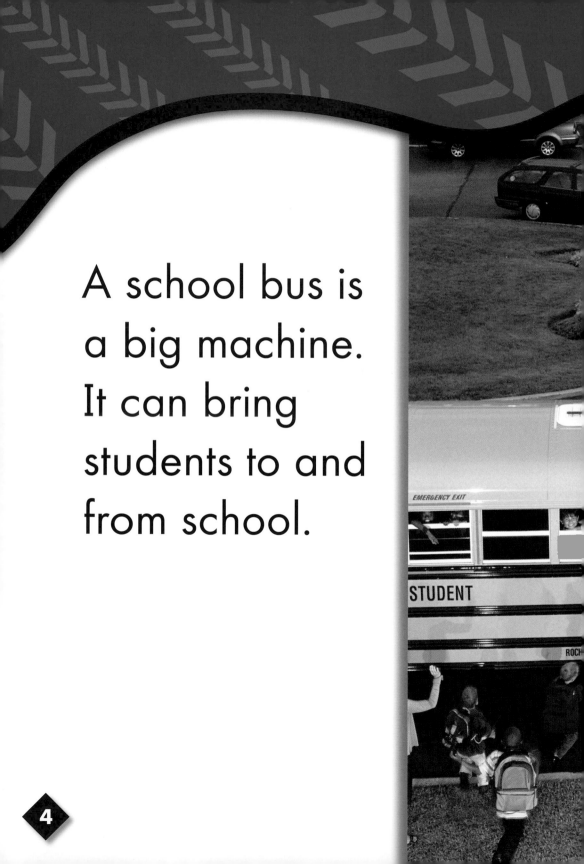

EMERGENCY EXIT

STUDENT

ROCH

A school bus
has a driver.

030269

THE RECOMMENDED MINIMUM TIRE AIR
PRESSURE FOR THIS POWER VEHICLE IS:
STEER AXLE
100 PSI   DRIVE AXLE (S)
                           PSI

The driver opens the door for students.

A school bus
has red lights.
These flash
when the
door is open.

A school bus
has a stop sign.
It sticks out
and tells other
drivers to wait.

A school bus has an **aisle**. The aisle runs between the seats.

15

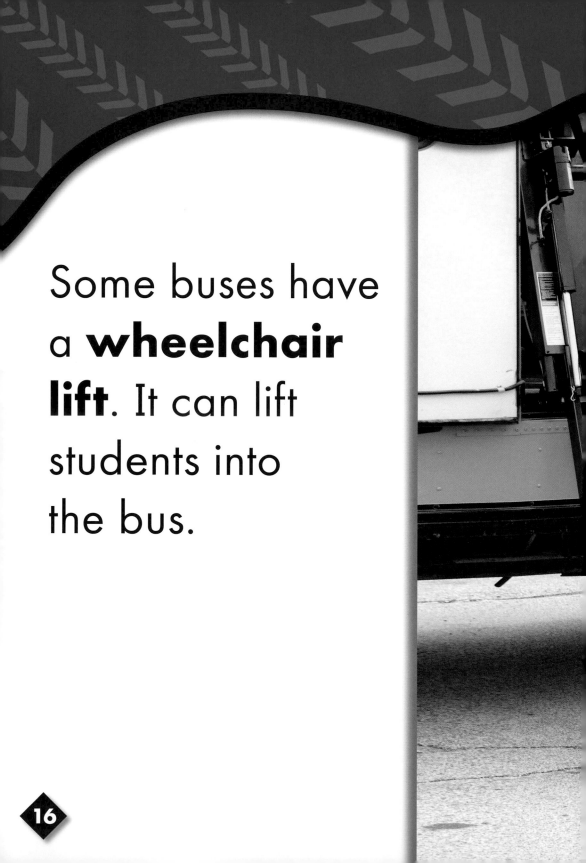

Some buses have a **wheelchair lift**. It can lift students into the bus.

School buses have an **emergency** door. Students can leave through this door in an emergency.

SCHOOL BUS

EMERGENCY EXIT

STATE LAW STOP
WHILE BUS IS

LOADING & UNLOADING

57

School buses
drop students
off at school.
Have fun!

Glossary

aisle—an area between seats where people can walk

emergency—a serious problem or time of danger

wheelchair lift—a tool used to raise a wheelchair into a vehicle

To Learn More

AT THE LIBRARY

Crews, Donald. *School Bus.* New York: Greenwillow Books, 1984.

Feldman, Heather. *My School Bus; A Book About School Bus Safety.* New York: Rosen, 2000.

Zuehlke, Jeffrey. *Buses.* Minneapolis, Minn.: Lerner, 2005.

ON THE WEB

Learning more about mighty machines is as easy as 1, 2, 3.

1. Go to www.factsurfer.com

2. Enter "mighty machines" into search box.

3. Click the "Surf" button and you will see a list of related web sites.

With factsurfer.com, finding more information is just a click away.

Index